Luca Petrov

Israel

Travel Guide

Catalog

Welcome to Israel

A Tapestry of Heritage

Israel: Where History and Diversity Unfold

While the world marvels at the cultural richness of iconic cities like Paris, Israel stands as a testament to a unique tapestry woven with history and diversity. Jerusalem, Tel Aviv, and Haifa are not just cities; they are living embodiments of a heritage that spans millennia. As a cradle of ancient civilizations and a modern melting pot, Israel offers a profound journey through time and culture.

Jerusalem: A City of Reverence and Contrasts

Jerusalem, with its labyrinthine alleys and sacred sites, invites you to explore a city where history and faith converge. The Western Wall, the Dome of the Rock, and the vibrant Mahane Yehuda Market are just a glimpse into the cultural wonders awaiting you.

Tel Aviv: The Modern Oasis by the Sea

Tel Aviv, often dubbed the "Mediterranean Miracle," is a vibrant hub of contemporary creativity. With its Bauhaus architecture, cutting-edge art scene, and bustling markets like Carmel and Florentin, Tel Aviv showcases Israel's modern face.

Haifa: Where Tradition Meets the Coast

Haifa, nestled between the hills and the Mediterranean, is a city of contrasts. The Baha'i Gardens, the German Colony, and the vibrant street art scene embody the harmonious blend of tradition and innovation that defines this coastal gem.

Diverse Delights

In a country where tradition and innovation dance in harmony, everyday life is a celebration of diversity. Israel, the birthplace of great minds like Einstein and the homeland of modern tech giants, is not only a historical treasure but also a vibrant tapestry of contemporary achievements.

From the bustling markets of Old Jaffa to the cutting-edge tech hubs in Herzliya, Israel's dedication to progress is evident. So, immerse yourself in the dynamic rhythm of Israeli life, savor the fusion of ancient traditions and modern flair, and embrace the vibrant mosaic that defines the Israeli way of life.

Culinary Kaleidoscope

Israel, often likened to a banquet table, beckons with a diverse array of flavors. From the aromatic spices of the Middle East to the fresh produce of local markets, every bite is a journey through the country's culinary kaleidoscope.

Indulge in the savory delights of falafel and shawarma on the bustling streets of Tel Aviv, or savor the aromatic spices of traditional dishes in the heart of Jerusalem's Old City. Israel's culinary scene is a blend of ancient traditions and contemporary innovation, with world-class chefs and street food vendors alike contributing to the delicious symphony of flavors.

Breathtaking Backdrops

Israel's allure extends beyond its historical and culinary treasures to embrace the breathtaking beauty bestowed by nature. From the rocky landscapes of the Negev Desert to the serene shores of the Sea of Galilee, Israel's diverse topography invites you to explore the great outdoors.

Embark on a hiking adventure in the rugged terrain of Ein Gedi, where desert waterfalls cascade through the canyons. Dive into the crystal-clear waters of the Red Sea in Eilat, or witness the sunrise from the ancient fortress of Masada. Israel's landscapes promise outdoor adventures as varied as its cultural heritage, inviting you to connect with nature in every corner of this captivating land.

Israel's Top 16 Must-Visit Destinations

1. Jerusalem's Old City

History:
Jerusalem's Old City dates back to ancient times, showcasing the footprints of various civilizations, including the Canaanites, Israelites, Babylonians, and Romans. Its historical and religious significance makes it a UNESCO World Heritage site.

Key Attractions:
Explore the labyrinthine streets, visit the Western Wall, and experience the spiritual ambiance. Don't miss the Church of the Holy Sepulchre, Dome of the Rock, and the Tower of David.

When to Visit:
Consider visiting during the spring or autumn to avoid the peak summer crowds. Major religious events may attract more visitors, so plan accordingly.

Contact Info:
Tourist Information Center: +972 2-627-1333
[Jerusalem Municipality](https://www.jerusalem.muni.il/en/)

Hidden Gems:

Explore the Armenian Quarter's hidden courtyards and discover the Cardo, an ancient Roman market street. Seek out local shops and cafes tucked away in the city's narrow alleys.

Culinary Delights:
Indulge in Middle Eastern cuisine at Azura or savor falafel at Lina's near Jaffa Gate.

2. Masada

History:
Masada, a fortress overlooking the Dead Sea, was the site of a heroic stand by Jewish rebels against Roman forces in the 1st century CE.

Key Attractions:
Ascend the mountain for panoramic views, explore the ancient palace, and learn about the history through the museum and archaeological remains.

When to Visit:
Visit during the cooler months, from autumn to spring, to make the ascent more comfortable.

Contact Info:
Masada Visitor Center: +972 8-658-4207

[Israel Nature and Parks Authority - Masada](https://www.parks.org.il/en/reserve-park/masada-national-park/)

Hidden Gems:
Explore the cisterns and water systems that highlight Masada's innovative engineering.

Culinary Delights:
Pack a picnic with local produce to enjoy against the breathtaking backdrop.

3. Tel Aviv's White City

History:
Tel Aviv's White City boasts a unique collection of over 4,000 Bauhaus-style buildings, designated as a UNESCO World Heritage site.

Key Attractions:
Stroll through Rothschild Boulevard, admire the architecture, and visit the Bauhaus Center to understand the significance of the White City.

When to Visit:
Tel Aviv is enjoyable year-round, but spring and fall offer pleasant weather for exploring on foot.

Contact Info:
Bauhaus Center: +972 3-516-6188
[Bauhaus Center Tel Aviv](http://www.bauhaus-center.com/)
Hidden Gems:
Explore the lesser-known Bauhaus buildings in the Lev Hair neighborhood for a quieter experience.
Culinary Delights:
Dine at one of the trendy cafes on Rothschild Boulevard or indulge in local dishes at Shuk HaCarmel.

4. The Dead Sea

History:
The Dead Sea, bordered by Jordan to the east and Israel to the west, has been renowned for its therapeutic properties since ancient times.
Key Attractions:
Float effortlessly in the mineral-rich waters, indulge in the famous mud treatments, and visit nearby attractions like Ein Gedi Nature Reserve.
When to Visit:
Year-round, but be cautious in the intense summer heat.
Contact Info:
Dead Sea Information Center: +972 8-995-3800
Hidden Gems:

Explore the natural wonders of Ein Bokek's hidden waterfalls and hike the trails of the Ein Gedi Nature Reserve.

Culinary Delights:

While culinary options may be limited directly at the Dead Sea, explore nearby towns for authentic Middle Eastern cuisine.

5. Haifa's Baha'i Gardens

History:

The Baha'i Gardens in Haifa are a sacred space for the Baha'i Faith, featuring meticulously landscaped terraces.

Key Attractions:

Wander through the terraces, visit the Shrine of the Bab, and enjoy panoramic views of Haifa and the Mediterranean.

When to Visit:

Spring and autumn offer pleasant weather. Check the Baha'i calendar for special events.

Contact Info:

Baha'i Gardens Visitor Center: +972 4-831-3131

[Baha'i Gardens Haifa](https://www.ganbahai.org.il/en/)

Hidden Gems:

Visit the nearby German Colony for charming streets, cafes, and boutiques.

Culinary Delights:
Explore the diverse culinary scene in the German Colony, offering a mix of international and local flavors.

History:
Mitzpe Ramon, perched on the edge of the Ramon Crater, is a small desert town known for its stunning geological formations.

Key Attractions:
Experience unparalleled stargazing, explore the unique landscapes of the Ramon Crater, and visit the visitor center for geological insights.

When to Visit:
Year-round, but cooler temperatures make outdoor activities more comfortable in the spring and autumn.

Contact Info:
Mitzpe Ramon Visitor Center: +972 8-658-8694

Hidden Gems:
Hike the Carpentry Trail for hidden viewpoints and unique rock formations.

Culinary Delights:
Discover local flavors at restaurants like Pundak Neot Smadar, offering a mix of traditional and modern dishes.

History:

Akko, or Acre, boasts a rich history, from ancient times through the Crusader period to Ottoman rule.

Key Attractions:

Walk through the well-preserved Crusader city, explore the underground tunnels of the Knights' Halls, and visit the vibrant Old City market.

When to Visit:

Spring and autumn offer pleasant weather for exploring the city on foot.

Contact Info:

Akko Tourist Information Center: +972 4-991-1375

Hidden Gems:

Explore the Templars' Tunnel, an underground passage connecting the port to the city.

Culinary Delights:

Indulge in fresh seafood at one of the Old City's authentic restaurants, such as Uri Buri.

History:
Caesarea, an ancient Roman city on the Mediterranean coast, showcases archaeological wonders.

Key Attractions:
Explore the well-preserved amphitheater, visit the ancient harbor, and wander through the remains of Herod's Palace.

When to Visit:
Visit in the cooler months to enjoy outdoor exploration comfortably.

Contact Info:
Caesarea National Park: +972 4-626-7080

Hidden Gems:
Visit the underwater archaeological park for a unique perspective on Caesarea's history.

Culinary Delights:
Dine at one of the seaside restaurants for a picturesque meal overlooking the Mediterranean.

History:
The Sea of Galilee, also known as Lake Kinneret, holds immense historical and religious significance, associated with biblical events.

Key Attractions:
Experience the tranquility of the freshwater lake, visit historic sites like Capernaum and the Mount of Beatitudes, and take a boat ride on the lake.

When to Visit:
Year-round, but spring and autumn offer pleasant weather for outdoor activities.

Contact Info:
Tourist Information Center - Tiberias: +972 4-672-1336

Hidden Gems:
Explore the Yigal Alon Museum, showcasing artifacts from the region's history.

Culinary Delights:
Sample local fish dishes in one of the lakeside restaurants for an authentic Galilean culinary experience.

History:
The Negev Desert, with its unique landscapes and historical sites, has been home to ancient civilizations and nomadic tribes.

Key Attractions:
Discover the unique landscapes, visit the Ramon Crater, and experience stargazing in the vast desert skies.

When to Visit:
Cooler months, from autumn to spring, are ideal for exploring the desert comfortably.

Contact Info:
Negev Desert Visitor Center: +972 8-628-0404

Hidden Gems:
Hike the Ein Avdat National Park for breathtaking canyon views and waterfalls.

Culinary Delights:
Experience Bedouin hospitality with traditional dishes at a local desert tent.

History:
Eilat, located on the Red Sea, has a history rooted in trade and is now a vibrant resort city.

Key Attractions:
Relax on the Red Sea beaches, go snorkeling or diving in the vibrant coral reefs of the Red Sea, and explore the underwater observatory.

When to Visit:
Eilat enjoys a warm climate year-round, but consider visiting in the cooler months for outdoor activities.

Contact Info:
Eilat Tourist Information Center: +972 8-634-9735

Hidden Gems:
Visit the Dolphin Reef, a unique eco-site where you can interact with dolphins in their natural habitat.

Culinary Delights:
Explore the diverse culinary scene, from seafood at Mul Hayam to international cuisine on the Eilat Promenade.

History:
Timna Park, located in the Negev Desert, is home to ancient copper mines dating back to the Bronze Age.

Key Attractions:
Marvel at the unique rock formations, visit the world's oldest copper mines, and explore the park's hiking trails.

When to Visit:
Visit in the cooler months to explore the park comfortably.

Contact Info:
Timna Park Visitor Center: +972 8-631-6756

Hidden Gems:
Hike the Hidden Valley trail for secluded views of the park's stunning landscapes.

Culinary Delights:
Pack a picnic to enjoy amidst the park's picturesque surroundings.

History:
Beit She'an, an archaeological site, showcases the remains of ancient civilizations, including the Romans and Byzantines.

Key Attractions:
Tour the well-preserved archaeological site, featuring theaters, bathhouses, and a colonnaded street.

When to Visit:
Spring and autumn are ideal for exploring the site comfortably.

Contact Info:
Israel Nature and Parks Authority - Beit She'an: +972 4-658-6219

Hidden Gems:
Explore the nearby Beit Alpha Synagogue, known for its well-preserved mosaic floor.

Culinary Delights:
While culinary options may be limited on-site, explore nearby towns for local dining experiences.

History:
Rosh Hanikra, on the northern border with Lebanon, features stunning white cliffs and sea caves.

Key Attractions:
Explore the sea caves, take a cable car ride to the grottos, and enjoy panoramic views of the Mediterranean.

When to Visit:
Visit during daylight hours to fully appreciate the natural beauty of the site.

Contact Info:
Rosh Hanikra Visitor Center: +972 4-982-3676

Hidden Gems:
Visit the beach below the cliffs for a secluded and peaceful experience.

Culinary Delights:
Explore local cafes in nearby towns like Nahariya for a taste of Mediterranean cuisine.

History:
The Mount of Olives, overlooking Jerusalem's Old City, has religious significance in Judaism, Christianity, and Islam.

Key Attractions:
Enjoy panoramic views of Jerusalem's Old City, visit the Chapel of the Ascension, and explore the historic Jewish cemetery.

When to Visit:
Anytime during the year, but sunrise and sunset provide particularly picturesque views.

Contact Info:
Jerusalem Municipality: +972 2-629-7777

Hidden Gems:
Visit the Church of All Nations and Dominus Flevit for lesser-known but stunning sites on the Mount.

Culinary Delights:
Explore nearby Jerusalem neighborhoods, like Mount Scopus, for local eateries offering a mix of cuisines.

History:
Jaffa's Old Port, one of the oldest ports in the world, has a history dating back thousands of years.

Key Attractions:
Wander through the ancient streets, visit art galleries, and enjoy the vibrant atmosphere of the Old Port.

When to Visit:
Daytime for exploring the historic sites, and evening for the lively atmosphere.

Contact Info:
Tel Aviv-Jaffa Municipality: +972 3-521-5200

Hidden Gems:
Explore the alleyways of the Flea Market for unique finds and local crafts.

Culinary Delights:
Indulge in fresh seafood at one of the portside restaurants, like Shaffa Bar.

Currency:
 - Israel uses the Israeli New Shekel (₪) as its official currency. ATMs are easily accessible at airports, cities, and towns. Credit cards are widely accepted in hotels and restaurants, providing convenient payment options for travelers.

Language:
 - Hebrew is the official language in Israel. While English is commonly spoken, especially in tourist areas, having a basic understanding of Hebrew phrases can enhance your interactions with locals and enrich your travel experience.

Visas:
 - Most travelers do not require a visa for stays up to 90 days in Israel. European Union (EU) nationals and citizens of several other countries typically enjoy visa-free entry. However, it's crucial to check specific visa requirements based on your nationality before your trip.

Money:
 - Israel's extensive network of ATMs allows easy access to cash. ATMs are available at airports, major cities, and towns. Credit cards are widely accepted in hotels and restaurants, offering secure and convenient payment options.

Mobile Phones:
 - European and Australian mobile phones generally work in Israel. Travelers from other regions should ensure their phones are set to roaming mode. For cost-effective local calls, consider purchasing a local SIM card upon arrival.

Time:
 - Israel operates on Israel Standard Time (IST), which is GMT/UTC plus two hours. Being aware of the time difference is essential for scheduling activities and making travel arrangements.

Room Tax:

- Visitors should be aware of a possible 'room occupancy tax,' typically ranging from ₪10 to ₪30 per night. Specific details can be found in local accommodations or on official websites.

Seasons:

- Israel experiences distinct seasons, each offering unique advantages:

   - *High Season (Apr–Oct):* Expect crowds at popular attractions. The weather is warm, and outdoor activities are enjoyable.

   - *Shoulder Season (Nov–Mar)*: Ideal for budget-conscious travelers. Weather varies, with cooler temperatures in the north and milder conditions in the south.

   - *Low Season (Jan–Feb):* Offers lower prices, but some attractions may have reduced hours. It's an excellent time for cultural events in major cities.

Emergency Numbers:

- In case of emergencies, remember these vital contact numbers in Israel:

   - *Ambulance: 101*
   - *Police: 100*
   - *Fire: 102*

- When calling from outside Israel, dial your international access code, followed by Israel's country code (972), and then the number (including the '0').

Useful Websites:

- While in Israel, utilize these helpful online resources:

   - *[Israel Railways](https://www.rail.co.il/en): O*fficial website for train travel information.

   - *[Israel Travel Center](https://www.goisrael.com):* Offers comprehensive travel information and resources.

   - *[Israel Antiquities Authority](http://www.antiquities.org.il):* Explore Israel's rich archaeological heritage.

   - *[Visit Tel Aviv](https://www.visit-tlv.com):* Discover the vibrant city of Tel Aviv.

Daily Costs:

Budget (Less than ₪200):

- Budget travelers can find affordable options in Israel. Hostel dorm beds range from ₪50 to ₪120. Meals at local eateries are generally reasonable, with prices for popular dishes ranging from ₪20 to ₪40.

Midrange (₪200–₪500):

- Midrange options provide a more comfortable experience. Double rooms in midrange hotels typically cost between ₪250 and ₪400. Enjoying meals at local restaurants may cost around ₪50 to ₪120 per person.

Top End (More than ₪500):

- Luxury travelers have a range of high-end options. Double rooms in upscale hotels can range from ₪400 to ₪800. Dining at top-end restaurants may cost between ₪150 and ₪300 per person, offering exceptional culinary experiences.

Opening Hours:

- Opening hours in Israel can vary based on the season. High-season hours generally apply from April to September, while low-season hours are in effect from October to March. Some general opening hours include:

- *Banks: 8.30am–12.30pm and 4–5pm, Sunday to Thursday*
- *Restaurants: Noon–3pm and 7–10pm*
- *Cafes: 8am–8pm*
- *Bars and clubs: 9pm–2am*
- *Shops: 9am–7pm, Sunday to Thursday, with shorter hours on Friday and Saturday.*

Arriving in Israel:

- Depending on your destination in Israel, you'll likely arrive at one of the major airports. Here are key transportation options from major airports to city centers:

- **Ben Gurion Airport (Tel Aviv):** Options include a train for ₪13.50 (every 30 minutes from 6am to midnight), a bus for ₪5.90 (running from 5.30am to 11pm), or a taxi with varied fares depending on the destination.

- **Sde Dov Airport (Tel Aviv):** Accessible by taxi or rideshare services, with fares depending on the destination.

- **Haifa Airport:** Transportation options include taxis or rideshare services.

With this practical information, you're well-equipped to explore Israel confidently, immersing yourself in its rich history, diverse culture, and stunning landscapes.

First Time in Israel?

 - Israel, with its diverse cultural influences, has varied dress codes. While Tel Aviv may be more casual, places like Jerusalem and Haifa may lean towards modest attire, especially in religious sites. Modesty is key when visiting religious places, with covered shoulders and knees often required. In urban areas, smart-casual attire is common. Comfortable shoes are crucial for exploring historical sites and diverse landscapes.

Sleeping:

 - Planning your stay in advance is advisable, especially during peak seasons or in popular destinations. Consider these accommodation options:
   - **Hotels:** Israel offers a range of hotels, from luxury to budget-friendly, providing diverse experiences.
   - **Guesthouses**: Experience local hospitality in guesthouses, often family-run and offering a more intimate stay.
   - **Hostels**: Ideal for budget-conscious travelers, hostels provide a social atmosphere and various room options.
   - **Vacation Rentals**: Explore the option of vacation rentals for a more independent stay, from city apartments to countryside retreats.

What to Pack:

 - Pack wisely for the diverse experiences Israel offers:
   - **Modest Attire:** Essential for visiting religious sites. Long skirts or pants, and tops covering shoulders are advisable.
   - **Sun Protection:** Israel's climate can be intense. Pack sunscreen, a hat, and sunglasses for protection.

- Electrical Adapter: Ensure your devices can be charged with the local power outlets.

- Comfortable Footwear: Especially important for exploring archaeological sites and diverse landscapes.

- Culinary Curiosity: Israel's cuisine is diverse; come with an open palate to savor local delights.

- Respectful Attitude: Embrace cultural diversity and be patient with occasional inefficiencies.

Money:

- Credit and debit cards are widely accepted, with Visa and MasterCard commonly recognized. American Express is accepted in larger establishments. ATMs are prevalent, but be aware of potential transaction fees. It's advisable to try multiple ATMs if your card is initially declined.

Bargaining:
- Bargaining is customary in markets. In smaller artisan shops, friendly bargaining may be acceptable, particularly for multiple purchases. However, it's generally not practiced in mainstream stores.

Tipping:
- Tipping is customary in restaurants. Consider these guidelines:

- *Restaurants:* Check if a service charge is included; otherwise, a tip of 10-15% is appropriate.

- *Taxis:* Optional, but rounding up to the nearest shekel is common.

- *Bars:* Similar to restaurants, tipping is customary, especially if drinks are brought to your table.

Etiquette:

- Israel values cultural respect. Consider these tips:

- Greetings: Use "shalom" as a universal greeting. A handshake is common, and cheek-kissing is typical among friends.

- Public Spaces: Use polite phrases like "slicha" (excuse me) and "bevakasha" (please) in crowded places.

- Religious Sites: Dress modestly, covering shoulders, torsos, and thighs. Show respect for religious customs and traditions.

These insights will help you navigate your first visit to Israel seamlessly, ensuring an enriching experience in this culturally diverse and historically significant country.

Jerusalem to Tel Aviv - 2 Weeks

Day 1 - 3: Jerusalem
Embark on your Israeli adventure in the historic city of Jerusalem. Spend three days exploring its sacred sites, from the Western Wall to the Church of the Holy Sepulchre. Immerse yourself in the vibrant atmosphere of Mahane Yehuda Market and discover the diverse neighborhoods that make up this ancient city.

Day 4 - 6: Dead Sea
Next, venture to the lowest point on Earth, the Dead Sea. Float effortlessly in its mineral-rich waters, indulge in renowned mud treatments, and absorb the therapeutic benefits of this unique natural wonder. Take a scenic drive along the shores and explore nearby attractions like Masada.

Day 7 - 9: Haifa and Akko (Acre)
Head to Haifa to explore the breathtaking Baha'i Gardens and enjoy panoramic views of the city and the Mediterranean. Continue to the well-preserved Crusader city of Akko, where underground tunnels and vibrant markets await your discovery.

Day 10 - 12: Galilee
Experience the tranquility of the Sea of Galilee, visiting historic sites and enjoying the natural beauty surrounding this freshwater lake. Explore the picturesque town of Tiberias and uncover the region's rich history, both ancient and modern.

Day 13 - 15: Tel Aviv
Conclude your journey in the dynamic city of Tel Aviv. Discover the unique Bauhaus architecture in the White City, relax on the Red Sea beaches, and explore the vibrant atmosphere of Jaffa's Old Port. Immerse yourself in the thriving culinary scene, from street food markets to upscale dining.

Day 1 - 3: Mitzpe Ramon
Begin your desert adventure in Mitzpe Ramon, a small town overlooking the Ramon Crater. Experience unparalleled stargazing, explore the unique landscapes, and marvel at the geological wonders of this desert region.

Day 4 - 6: Timna Park
Venture to Timna Park and marvel at the extraordinary rock formations. Visit the world's oldest copper mines and immerse yourself in the natural beauty of this desert landscape.

Day 7 - 9: Negev Desert
Continue your journey through the Negev Desert, discovering hidden gems like the ancient archaeological site of Beit She'an. Experience the vastness of the desert, visit the Ramon Crater, and appreciate the unique flora and fauna.

Day 10 - 12: Eilat
Relax on the pristine beaches of Eilat, explore vibrant coral reefs through snorkeling or diving, and visit the underwater observatory. Enjoy the lively atmosphere of this resort city nestled on the Red Sea.

Day 13 - 15: Rosh Hanikra and Northern Border
Conclude your nature expedition by exploring the stunning white cliffs and sea caves of Rosh Hanikra on the northern border with Lebanon. Take in the breathtaking views and savor the natural wonders of Israel's northern landscapes.

These thoughtfully crafted itineraries promise a diverse and immersive experience, showcasing the historical, cultural, and natural treasures of Israel. Enjoy your journey through this captivating and dynamic country!

The Culinary Calendar

In Israel, each season offers a distinctive array of flavors, allowing you to indulge in the country's culinary delights year-round. Here's an overview of the Israeli culinary calendar:

Spring (March - May)
Spring in Israel heralds fresh produce, featuring vibrant dishes with ingredients like artichokes and seasonal herbs. Special Passover dishes showcase the rich cultural and religious traditions. Food festivals, such as Tel Aviv's Eat Tel Aviv, highlight the diverse culinary scene.

Summer (June - August)
As summer arrives, Israeli cuisine bursts with the flavors of fresh tomatoes, cucumbers, and an abundance of colorful fruits. Explore the bustling markets, like Carmel Market in Tel Aviv, and savor refreshing dishes like watermelon with feta. Don't miss the opportunity to indulge in the vibrant street food culture.

Autumn (September - November)
Autumn brings a bounty of pomegranates, figs, and olives. Enjoy the olive harvest festivals in Galilee and Golan Heights. Delight in dishes like stuffed grape leaves (dolma) and explore wine festivals in regions like the Judean Hills, showcasing Israel's emerging wine scene.

Winter (December - February)
Israeli winters are a time for hearty stews, citrus fruits, and festive dishes. Embrace the holiday spirit with traditional Hanukkah treats like sufganiyot (jelly-filled doughnuts). Coastal cities like Jaffa offer seafood delicacies, providing a unique winter dining experience.

Falafel: A popular street food, deep-fried chickpea patties in a pita with fresh salads and tahini.

Sabich: A sandwich filled with fried eggplant, hard-boiled eggs, and various salads.

Hummus and Pita: Enjoy the iconic Middle Eastern dip with freshly baked pita bread.

Shawarma: Sliced meat (often lamb or chicken) wrapped in pita with tahini and vegetables.

Malabi: A creamy and refreshing milk pudding topped with rose water and chopped nuts.

Daring Tastings

Kubbeh: A dish made of semolina or bulgur filled with spiced meat, traditionally served in a warm broth.
Stuffed Vine Leaves (Warak Enab): Grape leaves filled with rice, pine nuts, and aromatic herbs.
Shakshuka: A breakfast favorite, eggs poached in a spicy tomato and pepper sauce.

Jerusalem Mixed Grill (Meorav Yerushalmi): A variety of grilled meats, often served in a pita with tahini and amba sauce.
Malawach: Layers of thin dough fried and served with various toppings, sweet or savory.
Knafeh: A sweet pastry made of thin noodle-like pastry soaked in sugar-based syrup, layered with cheese or semolina.

Local Delicacies

Embracing Israel's regional culinary diversity, each area boasts its own specialties:
1. Jerusalem & Surroundings: Enjoy traditional dishes like musakhan (roasted chicken with sumac and onions) and ka'ak (ring-shaped bread).
2. Tel Aviv & Coastal Areas: Dive into fresh seafood, with favorites like grilled sardines and fish shawarma. Explore the diverse array of international cuisines in Tel Aviv's vibrant food scene.
3. Galilee & Golan Heights: Savor dishes like stuffed grape leaves, labneh (strained yogurt), and grilled meats infused with regional herbs.
4. Negev Desert: Experience Bedouin hospitality with dishes like makluba (an inverted rice dish with meat and vegetables) and traditional Bedouin flatbreads.
5. Dead Sea Region: Indulge in artisanal dates and enjoy a culinary journey influenced by the rich minerals of the Dead Sea.
How to Eat & Drink Like an Israeli?
Mastering the art of eating and drinking like an Israeli is a cultural immersion. Here are some tips for an authentic Israeli dining experience:

Time of Eating

- **Breakfast:** Enjoy a leisurely Israeli breakfast with a spread of salads, cheeses, and bread.
- **Lunch:** Embrace the lively atmosphere of local markets or indulge in a falafel or sabich sandwich.

- Café Culture: Take part in the café culture, enjoying a strong espresso or refreshing mint tea.

- Dinner: Share a variety of small dishes, known as mezze, and savor the diverse flavors of Israeli cuisine.

Lehitra'ot! (Enjoy your meal in Hebrew)!

Adventure Activities in Israel

Israel, a country steeped in history and blessed with a diverse landscape, offers a rich tapestry of adventure activities. Let's delve into the in-depth details of these exhilarating experiences across the Israeli terrain.

1. Hiking

Israel's hiking trails span the entire country, offering diverse landscapes to explore.
- **Negev Desert**: Traverse the otherworldly landscapes of the Negev, with trails like the Red Canyon providing a mix of narrow passageways and towering cliffs.

- **Jerusalem Hills:** Experience ancient history while hiking through the hills surrounding Jerusalem. The Jerusalem Trail offers a unique blend of nature and historical sites.

- Galilee Region: Explore lush landscapes and historical sites in the Galilee, with trails leading to waterfalls, ancient ruins, and picturesque villages.

- Israel National Trail: This iconic trail stretches over 1,100 kilometers, from the northern border with Lebanon to the southern tip of Eilat, encompassing a variety of terrains.

Best Time: Spring and fall are ideal, avoiding the summer heat.

2. Cycling

Israel's cycling routes crisscross the country, combining scenic beauty with historical richness.

- Sea of Galilee: Pedal along the shores of the Sea of Galilee, enjoying the tranquil landscapes and stopping at historical sites like Capernaum.

- Negev Desert: Experience the vastness of the Negev on two wheels, with trails taking you through unique geological formations and Bedouin communities.

- Mediterranean Coast: Cycle along the Mediterranean coast, exploring ancient ports, vibrant markets, and modern beachfronts.

- Tel Aviv Urban Cycling: Discover the bustling city of Tel Aviv on a bike, exploring its neighborhoods, parks, and iconic landmarks.

Best Time: Winter and early spring for comfortable temperatures.

3. Rock Climbing

Israel's diverse topography offers rock climbing opportunities for all skill levels.
- **Negev Desert Cliffs**: Climb the dramatic cliffs of the Negev, with routes catering to beginners and advanced climbers alike.

- **Dead Sea Crags:** Experience unique climbing around the Dead Sea, combining breathtaking views with challenging ascents.
- **Golan Heights:** Explore the mountainous landscapes of the Golan Heights, known for its basalt cliffs and scenic routes.

Best Time: Cooler months from October to April for optimal conditions.

4. Diving

Israel's Red Sea coastline is a haven for diving enthusiasts.
- **Eilat:** Explore the vibrant coral reefs and underwater ecosystems of Eilat, known for its clear waters and diverse marine life.

- Red Sea Marine Reserve: Dive into the protected marine areas, witnessing colorful coral formations and a variety of sea creatures.
Best Time: Year-round, with warm waters and excellent visibility.

5. Windsurfing

Israel's coastlines, particularly the Mediterranean and Red Sea, offer prime windsurfing spots.
- Tel Aviv (Hilton Beach): Enjoy windsurfing against the backdrop of Tel Aviv's skyline and vibrant beach atmosphere.
- Eilat: Experience windsurfing in the Red Sea, with reliable winds and warm waters making Eilat a windsurfer's paradise.
Best Time: Summer months, especially from June to September, for optimal wind conditions.

6. Canyoning

Israel's canyoning adventures take you through hidden gems in nature.
- Ein Gedi Nature Reserve: Navigate through freshwater pools, waterfalls, and narrow canyons in this desert oasis.
- Golan Heights: Discover canyoning routes amidst the Golan's lush landscapes, combining water and challenging terrain.
Best Time: Spring and fall for moderate temperatures and flowing water.

7. Hot Air Ballooning

Soar above iconic landscapes for a bird's-eye view.
- Masada: Witness the sunrise over the ancient fortress of Masada, floating above the Judean Desert.
- Ramon Crater: Drift above the breathtaking Ramon Crater in the Negev, capturing panoramic views of its unique geological formations.
- Sea of Galilee: Enjoy picturesque views of the Sea of Galilee and surrounding landscapes from high above.

Best Time: Year-round, with each season offering a distinct panorama.

- **Spring and Fall**: Ideal for hiking, cycling, and canyoning with mild temperatures.
- **Summer:** Perfect for diving, windsurfing, and coastal activities.
- **Winter:** Excellent for rock climbing, hot air ballooning, and exploring diverse landscapes.

Israel's diverse adventure offerings provide a thrilling journey through history, nature, and adrenaline-pumping activities. Whether you're scaling cliffs, exploring underwater realms, or soaring in a hot air balloon, Israel invites you to embark on an adventure of a lifetime.

Early Settlements:

The history of Israel dates back to ancient times, with evidence of human habitation as early as the Paleolithic era. The region's significance is deeply rooted in its association with major historical and religious narratives.

Biblical Accounts:

The biblical narrative, particularly the Old Testament, plays a crucial role in shaping early Israeli history. Stories of patriarchs like Abraham, Isaac, and Jacob, as well as the Exodus from Egypt led by Moses, lay the foundation for the concept of the Promised Land.

Kingdom of Israel:

Around the 11th century BCE, the united Kingdom of Israel emerged under King Saul, followed by David and Solomon. This period is marked by the construction of the First Temple in Jerusalem, a symbol of Israelite religious and political unity.

Assyrian and Babylonian Exile:

However, the kingdom faced internal strife and eventually divided into the northern Kingdom of Israel and the southern Kingdom of Judah. Both kingdoms fell to successive invasions, leading to the Babylonian Exile, a critical event in Jewish history.

Return from Exile:

After the Babylonian Captivity, the Persian Empire allowed Jews to return to their homeland. This marked the beginning of the Second Temple period, during which the Second Temple was constructed in Jerusalem.

Hellenistic Influence:

Following the conquests of Alexander the Great, Israel came under Hellenistic influence. This period saw the clash between Hellenistic culture and Jewish traditions, leading to tensions within the region. The translation of the Hebrew Bible into

Greek, known as the Septuagint, reflects this cultural intersection.

Maccabean Revolt:

The Hellenistic influence escalated under the Seleucid Empire, leading to the oppression of Jewish religious practices. The Maccabean Revolt (167–160 BCE) marked a significant uprising against this oppression, resulting in the establishment of the Hasmonean dynasty.

Roman Rule:

In 63 BCE, Roman General Pompey conquered Jerusalem, incorporating Judea into the Roman Republic. This marked the beginning of Roman rule over the region. Despite initial autonomy under the rule of client kings, like Herod the Great, the Roman influence remained significant.

Life in Roman Judea:

During the Roman period, the region saw a complex tapestry of cultures and religions. The Pharisees, Sadducees, and Essenes emerged as influential religious sects. Meanwhile, Jesus of Nazareth, a central figure in Christianity, lived and preached in Judea during this time.

Destruction of the Second Temple:

One of the most pivotal events was the destruction of the Second Temple in 70 CE by the Romans under Titus. This event, along with the Bar Kokhba Revolt in 132–136 CE, had lasting consequences on Jewish identity and the landscape of the region.

Byzantine and Islamic Periods

Byzantine Era:

The Byzantine period began with the conversion of the Roman Empire to Christianity under Emperor Constantine in the 4th century. Israel, now part of the Eastern Roman Empire, witnessed the construction of numerous churches, including the Church of the Holy Sepulchre in Jerusalem.

The Persian Invasion:

In the early 7th century, the Persian Empire, under Khosrow II, invaded the region. This invasion weakened the Byzantine Empire and set the stage for the subsequent Islamic conquest.

Rise of Islam:

The Arab-Muslim forces, led by Caliph Umar, conquered Jerusalem in 637 CE. The Arab-Islamic rule brought a new era to the region, marked by religious tolerance, cultural flourishing, and advancements in science and philosophy. Jerusalem became a significant city in Islam, hosting the Dome of the Rock and Al-Aqsa Mosque.

The Umayyad and Abbasid Periods:

During the Umayyad Caliphate (661–750 CE), the administrative center moved to Damascus, but Jerusalem remained a prominent religious center. The Abbasid Caliphate (750–1258 CE) continued Islamic rule, fostering a vibrant cultural and intellectual environment.

Fragmentation and Crusades:

By the 11th century, the Seljuk Turks gained control, leading to conflicts with the Byzantine Empire and triggering the First Crusade in 1096. The Crusaders captured Jerusalem in 1099, establishing the Kingdom of Jerusalem. The Crusader rule continued until Saladin's recapture of Jerusalem in 1187.

Mamluk Rule:

The Mamluks, an Islamic dynasty, emerged victorious over the Crusaders. Their rule lasted from 1250 to 1517. During this period, Jerusalem's architectural landscape underwent changes, including the construction of the Mamluk structures seen in the Old City.

Ottoman Empire:

The Ottoman Empire, under Sultan Selim I, conquered the region in 1517. For centuries, the Ottomans ruled over Palestine, contributing to the diverse cultural and religious fabric of the area. This period saw demographic shifts and the emergence of distinct cultural traditions.

Ottoman Rule, British Mandate, and the Birth of Israel

Ottoman Rule:

The Ottoman Empire's control over the region persisted for centuries, shaping the social, economic, and political landscape. Jerusalem, a significant religious center, witnessed the construction of various structures, including the walls surrounding the Old City.

Demographic Changes:

During the Ottoman era, there were demographic shifts, with various ethnic and religious communities coexisting. Jerusalem's multicultural character became more pronounced, hosting Christian, Jewish, and Muslim quarters within the Old City.

19th-Century Changes:

The 19th century brought about transformative changes. European powers, particularly Britain and France, exerted influence, and Christian missionary activities increased. Jerusalem, with its religious significance, became a focal point for various geopolitical interests.

British Mandate:

After World War I, the League of Nations granted Britain the mandate to administer Palestine, including present-day Israel. The British Mandate, which began in 1920, faced resistance from both Jewish and Arab communities. Tensions escalated, and clashes became more frequent.

Balfour Declaration:

In 1917, the Balfour Declaration expressed British support for the establishment of a "national home for the Jewish people" in Palestine. This declaration significantly influenced the trajectory of the region, contributing to later conflicts.

Jewish Immigration and Arab Resistance:

Jewish immigration increased during the mandate period, leading to heightened tensions. Arab resistance, fueled by concerns about the establishment of a Jewish state, manifested in protests and uprisings, notably the Arab Revolt of 1936-1939.

Holocaust and Post-World War II:

The Holocaust during World War II underscored the urgent need for a Jewish homeland. After the war, waves of Jewish immigrants, including survivors of the Holocaust, sought refuge in Palestine. The British Mandate faced challenges in managing the competing demands of Jewish and Arab communities.

UN Partition Plan:

In 1947, the United Nations proposed a partition plan to divide Palestine into Jewish and Arab states, with Jerusalem as an international city. While the Jewish leadership accepted the plan, Arab leaders rejected it, leading to the 1948 Arab-Israeli War.

Establishment of Israel:

On May 14, 1948, David Ben-Gurion declared the establishment of the State of Israel. The declaration led to conflicts with neighboring Arab states, resulting in the first Arab-Israeli war. Despite facing military challenges, Israel survived and expanded its territory.

Armistice Agreements:

Armistice agreements were signed in 1949, delineating borders between Israel and its neighboring states. These borders, often referred to as the Green Line, shaped the geopolitical landscape for years to come.

Conclusion:

The establishment of Israel marked a pivotal moment in the region's history. The subsequent decades have been characterized by conflicts, negotiations, and efforts to address the complex issues surrounding the Israeli-Palestinian conflict. The historical journey of Israel is a testament to the intricate interplay of religious, cultural, and geopolitical factors in shaping the Middle East.

Other Useful Information

Israel provides a rich tapestry of accommodation options that cater to various tastes and budgets. From boutique hotels to unique desert lodges, beachfront resorts, and historic monasteries, the choices are diverse. Here's a comprehensive guide to help you navigate the accommodation landscape in Israel:

1. Advance Booking Strategies:

- **High Season Considerations:** During peak periods, such as Jewish holidays and major events like Jerusalem's International Film Festival, it's advisable to book in advance.

- **Popular Destinations:** Coastal areas like Tel Aviv during the summer and ski resorts like Mount Hermon in the winter experience high demand. Booking ahead is crucial.

2. Seasonal Nuances:

- **Tourist Peaks:** Israel experiences tourist peaks during Jewish holidays, especially Passover and Sukkot, as well as Christmas and Easter. Prices tend to surge during these times.

- **Regional Variation:** Coastal cities may see peak demand in the summer, while the Negev Desert may attract more visitors in the cooler months. Consider the seasonal fluctuations based on your destination.

3. Geographical Price Differences:

- **City-Centric Pricing**: Accommodation costs in major cities like Jerusalem and Tel Aviv may differ significantly from smaller towns or rural areas.

- **Budget Planning:** A midrange option in the bustling city of Haifa might be comparable to a more luxurious choice in the tranquil Galilee region. Take regional price variations into account.

4. Meal Packages and Board Options:

- Half and Full Board: Some accommodations provide meal packages. Half-board typically includes breakfast and one additional meal, while full board includes all three. Inquire about these options for added convenience.

5. Negotiation Tactics in Low Season:

- Low-Season Deals: During the low season, particularly at smaller establishments, consider negotiating for discounts, especially for extended stays.

- Last-Minute Deals: Explore last-minute deals on online platforms like Booking.com and Airbnb for potential cost savings.

6. Payment and Confirmation:

- Credit Card Protocol: Many hotels may require a credit card for reservation confirmation, particularly at midrange and budget establishments. Be mindful of cancellation policies to avoid charges.

Types of Accommodation:

1. Boutique Guesthouses (Similar to B&Bs):
- Israel has a burgeoning boutique guesthouse scene, offering unique stays in urban and rural settings. Prices range from approximately ₪150 to ₪600 per person.

2. Camping Grounds:
- Various well-equipped campgrounds are scattered across Israel, especially near nature reserves and national parks. Prices fluctuate, with high season rates ranging from ₪30 to ₪100 per person.

3. Historic Monasteries and Convents:
- Some monasteries and convents in Israel offer rooms to tourists. Prices are often reasonable, and early curfews might be in place. Explore options through MonasteryStays.com and local listings.

4. Hostels:
- Affiliated with Hostelling International, Israeli hostels require a valid membership card. Prices for dormitory beds range from

₪50 to ₪120 per night, including breakfast. Single and double rooms are also available.

5. Hotels:
   - Graded from one to five stars, hotel prices can vary widely. In major cities, a single room may start from ₪150, while double rooms typically range from ₪250 upwards, depending on location, season, and quality.

6. Mountain Lodges:
   - The mountainous regions, including the Golan Heights, offer lodges typically open from spring to fall. Prices range from ₪80 to ₪200 per person, including breakfast. Reservations are crucial.

7. Rental Accommodations:
   - Short-term rentals in cities like Tel Aviv can be found on platforms like Airbnb. Prices vary, but expect to pay around ₪1,500 to ₪4,000 per month for a small apartment.

8. Resort Villas:
   - Agencies like Israel Vacation Homes provide villa rentals in scenic locations. Prices can vary widely based on size, location, and amenities, ranging from ₪500 to ₪3,000 per night.

Additional Considerations:

- **Accommodation Tax:** Introduced in 2011, Israel has an accommodation tax, usually ranging from ₪5 to ₪20 per night per room. Some places exempt children from this tax.

- **Local Expertise**: Tourist offices and online platforms such as Booking.com, Airbnb, and local rental agencies can assist in finding accommodation tailored to your needs.

Navigating Israel's diverse accommodation options allows you to customize your stay, ensuring a memorable and comfortable experience throughout your exploration of this multifaceted country.

Customs Regulations in Israel

When embarking on a journey to Israel, understanding the customs regulations and relevant information is crucial. Here's a comprehensive guide to help you navigate customs, duty-free allowances, and practical details during your visit:

Duty-Free Opportunities:

While the European Union's duty-free sales no longer apply in Israel, there are opportunities for tax-free shopping in certain locations. Airports may offer tax-free goods, including electronics, perfumes, and luxury items.

Duty-Free Allowances for Non-Israeli Visitors:

If you're arriving in Israel from a non-EU country, certain duty-free allowances apply. Here's an overview:

- *Spirits: 1 liter (or 2 liters of wine)*
- *Perfume: 50 grams*
- *Eau de Toilette: 250 milliliters*
- *Cigarettes: 200*
- *Other Goods: Up to a total value of €175*

Goods exceeding these limits should be declared upon arrival, with appropriate duties paid. Non-Israeli citizens departing Israel after high-value purchases may reclaim value-added tax, offering savings on significant items.

Discount Opportunities:

- **Age-Based Discounts:** Travelers in Israel can explore age-based discounts. Those under 18 and over 65 may enjoy free admission to various attractions. Visitors aged 18 to 25 often qualify for discounts, sometimes exclusive to EU citizens.

- **Special Discount Cards:** Certain cities or regions offer special discount cards. For instance, cards like the Jerusalem Pass provide free or reduced admission to museums. Combination tickets are available in different locations, providing cost savings for multiple attractions.

- **Youth Cards:** The Israeli youth card offers discounts on accommodations, museums, restaurants, and more. Students, teachers, and youth cardholders can find savings, contributing to a budget-friendly travel experience.

Electricity Standards:

- **Voltage:** Israel follows the European standard of 220-230V with a frequency of 50Hz.

- Plugs: Wall outlets typically accommodate plugs with two or three round pins, with the latter grounded and the former ungrounded.

Embassies and consulates are vital resources for travelers. Some contacts for various embassies and consulates in Israel include:
- *Australian Embassy/Consulate: Tel Aviv*
- *Austrian Embassy/Consulate: Tel Aviv*
- *Canadian Embassy: Tel Aviv*
- *French Embassy/Consulate: Tel Aviv and Jerusalem*
- *German Embassy/Consulate: Tel Aviv and Jerusalem*
- *Irish Embassy: Tel Aviv*
- *Japanese Embassy/Consulate: Tel Aviv*
- *Dutch Embassy/Consulate: Tel Aviv*
- *New Zealand Embassy/Consulate: Tel Aviv*
- *Slovenian Embassy/Consulate: Tel Aviv*
- *Swiss Embassy/Consulate: Tel Aviv*
- *UK Embassy/Consulate: Tel Aviv*
- *US Embassy/Consulate: Tel Aviv and Jerusalem*

Understanding these details will empower travelers in Israel, ensuring a smooth experience with customs, discounts, and access to embassy support when needed.

Money Matters in Israel

When exploring the beautiful landscapes of Israel, having a solid understanding of the local currency and practical financial aspects is essential. Here's a comprehensive guide to managing your money in Israel:

Currency:

Israel's official currency is the New Israeli Shekel (NIS). Banknotes are available in denominations of NIS 200, 100, 50, and 20, while coins come in denominations of NIS 10, 5, and 1, as well as 50 and 10 agorot.

ATMs & Credit Cards:

- ATMs (Bankomat): Israel boasts a widespread network of ATMs, making it convenient to access local currency. International credit and debit cards with major logos such as Visa and MasterCard are widely accepted.

- Credit Cards: Major credit cards are commonly used for payments at hotels, restaurants, shops, and various establishments. Visa and MasterCard are prevalent, but it's advisable to inquire about specific card acceptance.

- Bank Charges: Check with your bank regarding fees for foreign transactions. Commonly, banks charge around 2-3% for each foreign transaction, and additional fees may apply to ATM withdrawals.

Money Changers:

Currency exchange services are available at banks, post offices, and authorized money changers. While banks and post offices often provide favorable rates, money changers might offer extended hours for convenience. Be aware of potential commissions and less advantageous rates at certain exchange offices.

Taxes & Refunds:

Israel imposes Value Added Tax (VAT), known as Ma'am, at a standard rate of 17%. As a non-resident, you may be eligible for a VAT refund on purchases exceeding a certain amount. Ensure you follow these steps:

1. Complete a refund form at the point of purchase.
2. Have the form validated by Israeli customs upon departure.
3. Refunds are typically processed back to your credit card.

Tipping:

Tipping practices in Israel are akin to those in many Western countries. While it's not mandatory, tipping for good service is appreciated. Here's a general guide:

- Restaurants: 10-15% is customary if a service charge is not included.

- Bars: A small tip, around NIS 5-10, is acceptable for table service.

- Hotels: Tip around NIS 5-10 for porter assistance or other services.

- Taxis: Rounding up the fare is customary.

Israel's postal system, Israel Post (www.israelpost.co.il), provides reliable mail services. Stamps (temaniot) can be purchased at post offices. Postage costs vary based on the letter's weight, size, and destination. The priority mail service ensures delivery within a few days, both locally and internationally.

Understanding these aspects will help you manage your finances effectively during your visit to Israel, ensuring a smooth and enjoyable experience.

Public Holidays in Israel

When planning your visit to Israel, it's crucial to be aware of the national public holidays, as they may impact your travel itinerary. Key public holidays in Israel include:

- New Year's Day (Rosh Hashanah) - Date varies (usually in September)
- Yom Kippur (Day of Atonement) - Date varies (usually in September)
- Sukkot - Date varies (usually in September/October)
- Simchat Torah - Date varies (usually in October)
- Hanukkah - Date varies (usually in December)
- Tu BiShvat - Date varies (usually in January/February)
- Purim - Date varies (usually in February/March)
- Passover (Pesach) - Date varies (usually in March/April)
- Independence Day (Yom Ha'atzmaut) - 14th day of Nisan in the Hebrew calendar (usually in April/May)
- Jerusalem Day (Yom Yerushalayim) - 28th day of Iyar in the Hebrew calendar (usually in May)
- Shavuot - 6th day of Sivan in the Hebrew calendar (usually in May/June)
- Tisha B'Av - Date varies (usually in July/August)
- Islamic New Year (Ras as-Sanah al-Hijriyah) - Date varies (based on the Islamic lunar calendar)
- Eid al-Fitr - Date varies (celebrated at the end of Ramadan)

- Eid al-Adha - Date varies (celebrated in connection with the Hajj pilgrimage)

It's important to note that some holidays are based on the Hebrew calendar or the Islamic lunar calendar, so their dates vary each year.

Telephone and Communication in Israel

Ensuring smooth communication during your stay in Israel involves considering the following:

- **Domestic Calls:** Israel has an area code system integral to telephone numbers. Mobile phone numbers typically start with a specific prefix. Familiarize yourself with the system for easy communication.

- **International Calls:** Opt for cost-effective communication through computer programs and apps like Skype and Viber for international calls. Alternatively, look for affordable call centers in major cities.

- **Mobile Phones:** Israel uses GSM 900/1800, compatible with European and Australian phones. Ensure your mobile phone is compatible or unlock it for use with an Israeli SIM card. Tourists can easily find prepaid SIM cards.

- **Payphones & Phone Cards:** Payphones in Israel accept phone cards available at post offices, tobacconists, and newsstands. Be mindful of expiration dates and consider Telecom Israel for phone card purchases.

- **Time Zone:** Israel operates on Israel Standard Time (IST), which is UTC+2. Note that Israel observes daylight-saving time, usually starting on the Friday before the last Sunday in March and ending on the last Sunday in October.

Understanding these details will enhance your connectivity and overall experience during your travels in Israel.

Before embarking on your journey to Israel, it's crucial to grasp the visa and residency regulations to ensure a smooth and legally compliant stay. Here's a comprehensive overview:

1. Visa Exemptions for Tourists:

- Israel allows visa exemptions for citizens from various countries, including Australia, Brazil, Canada, Italy, Japan, New Zealand, and the USA. Travelers from these countries can typically stay for up to 90 days without a visa. However, specific regulations may apply, especially if you plan to travel to other destinations afterward.

2. Work and Study Visas:

- If you intend to work or study in Israel, you'll need to obtain the relevant visa.

- Work visas are generally issued in coordination with a job offer from an Israeli employer, and the application process may involve providing proof of employment, qualifications, and other supporting documents.

- Study visas are necessary for those planning to enroll in Israeli educational institutions. Proof of acceptance, payment of fees, and evidence of financial means may be required.

3. Residency for Non-Israeli Citizens:

- Non-Israeli citizens, including those from non-EU countries, may apply for residency based on various criteria, such as employment, marriage to an Israeli citizen, or being a child of an Israeli citizen.

- Each category has specific requirements, and the application process can vary. It's advisable to consult with the relevant authorities or official sources for the most accurate and up-to-date information.

4. Temporary Resident Status:

- Individuals residing in Israel on a temporary basis for work or other reasons may be granted temporary resident status. This status is usually valid for a specified period and may be subject to renewal.

5. Tourist Stays and Extensions:

- Tourists visiting Israel are typically granted a specific period of stay upon entry. It's essential to adhere to this timeframe to avoid legal complications.

- If you wish to extend your stay for tourism purposes, you may need to apply for an extension through the appropriate channels.

6. Consular Services:

- For comprehensive and accurate information on visa requirements and residency, it's recommended to contact the Israeli embassy or consulate in your home country or visit the official website www.israelvisa.com for the latest updates.

Understanding the intricacies of visa and residency regulations in Israel is essential for a hassle-free and compliant stay. Always refer to official sources and seek professional advice when needed to ensure your travel plans align with legal requirements.

Traveling to Israel:

Israel boasts a well-developed transportation infrastructure, providing diverse options for travelers to access the country seamlessly. Whether by air, land, or sea, Israel's connectivity facilitates easy exploration of its attractions.

By Air:

Israel is served by major international airports, with Ben Gurion Airport in Tel Aviv being the primary gateway. Other significant airports include Sde Dov Airport in Tel Aviv and Ovda Airport near Eilat. Airlines such as El Al, Israel's national carrier, along with international carriers, ensure comprehensive air connectivity.

Intra-regional flights cater to various Israeli cities, and airlines like El Al, Arkia, and Israir offer domestic services. Budget airlines may provide affordable options for those exploring different parts of the country.

Entering the Country:

- Visitors to Israel typically require a valid passport. Check visa requirements based on your nationality before traveling.
- Upon arrival, travelers must comply with Israeli immigration procedures, which may include passport checks and completion of entry forms.
- Adherence to local laws, including the requirement to carry identification, is essential, and it's advised to cooperate with authorities as needed.

By Land:

Israel's land connections are well-established, allowing easy access from neighboring countries:

- Jordan: Crossings include the King Hussein Bridge near Jericho and the Arava Crossing near Eilat.

- Egypt: The Taba Border Crossing facilitates travel between Eilat and the Sinai Peninsula.

- The West Bank: Various checkpoints enable travel between Israel and the West Bank, with specific considerations and regulations.

By Bus:

Buses provide an economical mode of transport within Israel, with routes connecting major cities. Companies like Egged and Dan offer extensive bus services, making it a practical option for budget-conscious travelers.

By Car and Motorcycle:

- Renting a car or motorcycle is a popular choice for exploring Israel's diverse landscapes.
- Ensure compliance with local driving regulations, and carry necessary documentation, including proof of ownership and insurance.

By Train:

Israel's rail network connects key cities, offering an efficient and eco-friendly travel option. While train travel may not cover all regions, it's a viable choice for certain routes, producing fewer carbon emissions compared to other modes of transportation.

By Sea:

Israel's coastal location makes sea travel an option:

- Ferries connect Israel with neighboring countries, with routes varying in frequency and availability.
- Some ferry services cater to transporting vehicles, offering an alternative for those looking to explore Israel by road.

For updated information on transportation services and schedules, it's recommended to check with relevant authorities, transportation companies, or official travel resources.

Understanding the diverse transportation options ensures that travelers can navigate Israel conveniently, creating a memorable and hassle-free experience.

Getting Around Israel

Once you've landed in Israel, you'll find a variety of transportation options to explore the country efficiently. From domestic flights to bicycles, boats, buses, taxis, trains, and rental vehicles, Israel offers a diverse range of choices for travelers.

By Air:

While Israel is relatively compact, domestic flights are available. Arkia and Israir are among the local carriers, providing connections to Eilat and other destinations. Ben Gurion Airport, located near Tel Aviv, is the main international gateway.

Price Range: Domestic flight prices can vary, with one-way tickets typically ranging from ₪150 to ₪500, depending on the destination and the airline.

By Bicycle:

Cycling is a popular mode of transportation in Israel. Visitors can bring their own bikes or rent locally. Certain areas may have designated cycling paths, providing an enjoyable and eco-friendly way to discover the landscape.

Price Range: Bike rentals can range from ₪30 to ₪100 per day, depending on the type of bicycle and its features.

By Boat:

For island destinations such as Eilat and others along the Mediterranean coast, various ferry services are available. These can include larger ferries for vehicles and smaller ferries or hydrofoils for passengers. Prices may vary based on the type of vessel and the size of your vehicle.

Price Range: Ferry prices vary, with passenger ferry tickets ranging from ₪50 to ₪150. Vehicle transport prices can range from ₪150 to ₪500, depending on the size of the vehicle.

By Bus and Metro:

Israeli cities feature comprehensive bus and, in some cases, metro systems. Major cities like Tel Aviv and Jerusalem have efficient public transportation networks, making it convenient for travelers to explore urban areas.

Price Range: Bus and metro tickets are generally affordable, ranging from ₪5 to ₪20 per trip, depending on the distance traveled.

By Taxi:

Taxis are readily available in cities and can be hailed on the street or called through a taxi service. While taxis may have meters, it's essential to confirm the fare structure. Tipping is customary but not mandatory.

Price Range: Taxi fares start around ₪12 to ₪20, with an additional ₪4 to ₪8 per kilometer. Tipping is generally around 10%.

By Train:

Israel Railways operates the country's train services, connecting major cities. The train system provides a comfortable and scenic way to travel, with routes offering views of Israel's diverse landscapes.

- Train Classes and Costs:

 - Trains typically have both standard and first-class seating, with varying ticket prices.

 - The cost of train tickets can depend on factors such as class, travel time, and whether tickets are booked in advance.

- Train Passes:

 - For those planning extensive train travel, Israel Railways offers various ticket options, including monthly subscriptions and discounts for seniors and students.

Price Range: Standard train tickets range from ₪15 to ₪60, while first-class tickets can be between ₪40 and ₪120, depending on the route and class.

By Car:

Driving in Israel is a convenient option for those looking to explore beyond major cities. The road network includes highways, and tolls may apply. Car rental companies operate in major cities and at airports.

- Driving Tips:

  - Be aware of traffic regulations and speed limits.

  - Parking in city centers may require payment, and Zona a Traffico Limitato (restricted traffic zones) exist in some areas.

  - Fuel stations are widely available, and fuel prices can vary.

Price Range: Car rental prices start at approximately ₪100 per day, varying based on the vehicle type and rental duration. Fuel costs are around ₪6 per liter.

By Motorcycle and Scooter:

Motorcycles and scooters are common in Israel, especially in urban areas. Rental services are available, offering an agile means of transportation.

Price Range: Motorcycle and scooter rentals range from ₪50 to ₪150 per day, depending on the model and features.

Renting a Vehicle:

Renting a car or motorcycle requires a valid driver's license, identification or passport, and, for car rentals, a credit card. Minimum age requirements may apply, and it's crucial to understand local traffic rules.

Israel's rich history, diverse landscapes, and cultural attractions make it an exciting destination to explore. Whether you're wandering through ancient sites, relaxing on the beaches, or experiencing the vibrant city life, Israel's transportation options ensure a seamless and memorable journey with prices that cater to various budgets.

Copyright and Disclaimer:

Images Source:

Pixbay: (https://pixabay.com/)

All images' rights belong to their respective owners.

For detailed image licensing terms and conditions, kindly refer to the respective image sites' licensing terms and conditions.

Disclaimer:

This disclaimer is hereby presented to inform users of the "Israel Travel Guide" (henceforth referred to as "the Guide") of the terms and conditions of its use. By accessing or using this travel guide, you agree to the following conditions:

1. General Information: The Guide is created for informational purposes and offers travel-related content and advice related to Israel. It aims to provide general information and suggestions, which may not always be up to date. It is not a substitute for professional travel advice.

2. Accuracy of Information: While we strive to provide accurate and current information, we make no representations or warranties of any kind, expressed or implied, about the completeness, accuracy, reliability, suitability, or availability of the information, products, services, or related graphics contained in the Guide. Users should verify information independently before relying on it.

3. Liability Disclaimer: The author and the publisher of this Guide will not be liable for any loss or damage, including but not limited to indirect or consequential loss or damage, or any loss or damage whatsoever arising from loss of data or profits arising out of, or in connection with, the use of this Guide.

4. Third-Party Content: The Guide may include links to third-party websites or services related to Israel. We have no control over the nature, content, and availability of these sites and services. Inclusion of any links does not imply a recommendation or endorsement of the views expressed within them.

5. Safety and Legal Compliance: It is the user's responsibility to exercise caution, act in accordance with local laws and regulations, and ensure personal safety when engaging in any suggested activities or traveling in Israel.

6. Personal Responsibility: Users are solely responsible for their decisions and actions based on the information and advice provided in this Guide. The author and the publisher are not responsible for users' choices or outcomes related to travel or other activities in Israel.

By accessing or using this Israel Travel Guide, you agree to be bound by this disclaimer. If you disagree with any part of these terms and conditions, you are not allowed to use this Guide.

Milton Keynes UK
Ingram Content Group UK Ltd.
UKHW020714011223
433473UK00010B/151